There are about 50 million sheep in New Zealand (over 12 for every person!). They're reared for meat or fleece or a combination of both. Next to the Romney breed, the Cheviot is one of the most common. This one *(opposite below)*, a ewe in full fleece, has recently lambed, and rests, like a matriarch, eyes half closed in the spring sunshine. Lambing takes place mainly from October through to December when the pastures appear to teem with ewes and their leggy offspring. All too soon, it seems, they grow up and within a few weeks start to look like their parents *(right)* – larger and less inclined to bounce and play.

The black-faced South Suffolk *(opposite top)* is one of the more unusual breeds, while the Merino, a characteristically spiral-horned, strong, hardy sheep much suited to the high, rugged alpine slopes of the South Island is grown for its fine wool. In this photograph *(below)* élite Merinos are being judged for top awards at an annual Canterbury Agricultural and Pastoral Show.

Millions of sheep must be shorn of their wool when their fleeces are grown and so gangs of shearers move around the country, from farm to farm, to do the work. Typically they're strong men of good humour *(below)* and proud of their craft, able to shear 200-300 sheep a day. At Te Kuiti, in the North Island, which claims to be the 'Shearing Capital of the World' the iconic New Zealand shearer is honoured by this seven-metre-high statue *(left)*.

While one would expect to see vast flocks of sheep ranging on remote South Island hillsides such as above the Clutha River near Tuapeka, in inland Otago *(overleaf)*, it comes as a surprise to see them grazing the slopes of Maungakiekie just a few kilometres from the centre of Auckland *(below right)*. But it would come as no surprise should a farmer and his dog appear anywhere on an all-terrain vehicle, repairing fences, checking livestock or obligingly posing for photographs . . . *(opposite top)*.

There are about 10 million cattle in New Zealand, half of which are farmed mainly for their meat and the other half for their dairy products: milk, butter and cheeses. The Simmental *(left)* which has become increasingly popular, serves a dual purpose providing milk and beef, whereas the large, creamy white Charolais *(opposite below)* a breed originating from France, is grown only for its meat.

The rich milk of Jersey cows makes excellent butter and cheeses; there's probably no sight more charming than a bunch of new season's Jerseys *(opposite top)* who will readily, and with great patience and curiosity, line up for a group portrait.

Cattle farmers, so often remote from their neighbours, welcome the opportunity to compare notes as they watch or take part in the bidding at auction sales *(below)* regularly mounted by stock and station agents.

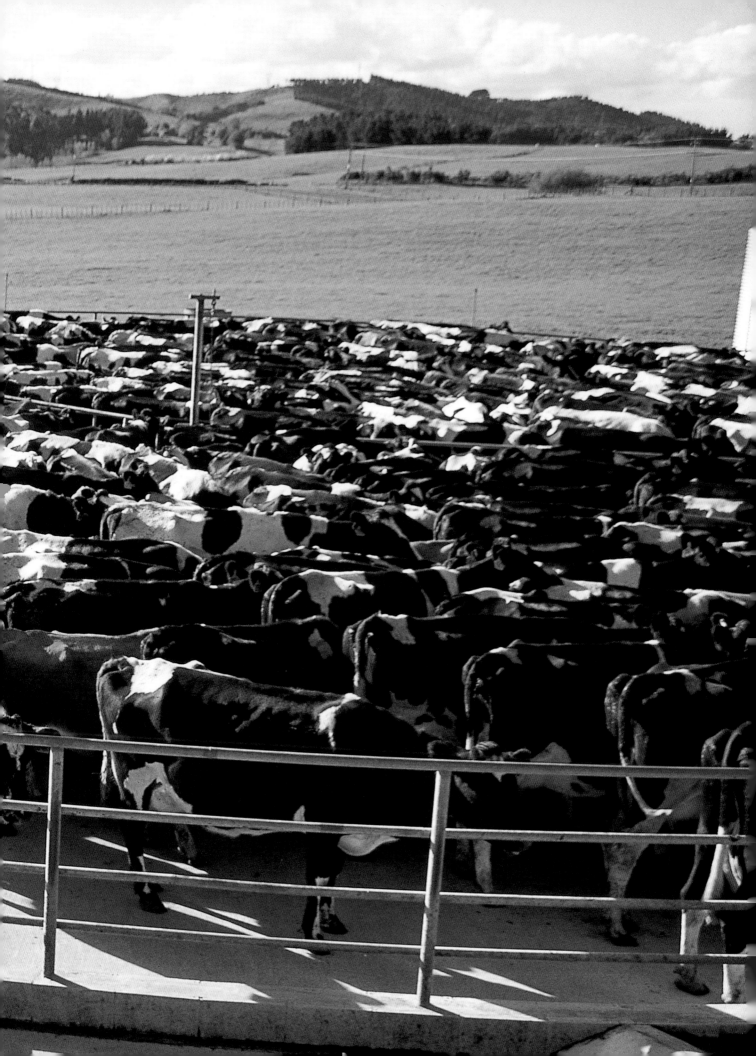

(Previous pages) At a large organic dairy farm south of Auckland, as many as 500 milking cows are held in this yard before they enter a rotary parlour capable of holding 50 cattle at a time. As the platform rotates - accommodating 400 cows an hour - it requires only two people to attach and detach the udder cups *(opposite)*. The main breed from which milk is supplied to towns and cities is the distinctively black and white Friesian *(right)* which, cow for cow, gives a much higher yield than the Jersey though not as high a butterfat content.

Where farms in country areas straddle a highway it's not unusual for traffic to be held up while herds are driven to and from their milking sheds *(below)*. Motorists are usually content to watch the passing plodders driven by a farmer on his four-wheel ATV, perhaps helped by his wife and children, and almost invariably a fast-moving dog or two.

New Zealand prides itself on being 'clean and green' and nothing more emphasises that claim than the brilliance of spring pastures and crops. The young wheat growing in the fields of the South Island's Canterbury Province *(left)* is green with promise. Its already generous seed heads will turn to gold as they ripen in the summer sunshine.

Maize, also known as sweet corn (the corn that in the song grows 'as high as an elephant's eye'), while found in many lowland areas, is a particular feature of the Waikato, in the North Island *(opposite),* where this dense crop is well over two metres high.

Perhaps the biggest surprise, in a landscape whose colours are usually tertiary greens, browns and silver-greys, is to suddenly come upon a field of oilseed rape or canola *(below)* a startling canary yellow as it contrasts sharply against the blue of the sky.

Kiwifruit, once known as Chinese Gooseberries, dull brown on the outside but with luscious emerald green or golden flesh rich in vitamin C, have been cultivated and greatly improved for many years and are now one of the country's best known export fruits. They grow on vines trained along terraces such as at Riverhead, near Auckand *(opposite)*. These fruit, almost ripened, are at harvesting point and ready to go to the packing sheds.

As they mature, grapes become irresistible to small birds, thus wine-vine growers resort to rows and rows of protective netting at this vineyard north-west of Auckland *(right)*. Even more elaborate precautions are taken in cherry orchards. This one in Roxburgh, Central Otago, *(below)* has two kinds of high-level covers in place: one is made of netting to foil cherry-loving birds at ripening time, the other, like a tarpaulin, is to protect the crop from rain and hail.

Often seen lining roadsides or separating paddocks are flowering pampas grasses, their plumes mostly a subtle creamy light brown colour although there are others in pale green and yellow. Beyond the clumps *(above)* growing in the North Island's Bay of Plenty, is a new orchard of avocado trees, carefully planted within screens to shield them from the wind. The most common is the pear-shaped variety Haas.

There are few sights prettier than an apple orchard with its trees in full blossom. What can't be conveyed in this picture *(opposite)* is the orchardist's delight in the floral perfume or in watching and hearing the bees of springtime humming as they harvest its pollen. Later the Braeburn apples will be ready for picking, the highest branches being reached by power ladder *(left)*, which is manoeuvred by foot controls so as to leave the picker's hands free.

(Overleaf) Kiwifruit orchards in autumn at Riwaka in the South Island's Nelson Province.

There's more to the animals of rural New Zealand than cattle and sheep although other creatures are here in fewer numbers. Pigs, for example: there are wild ones and domestic; you might never catch a casual glimpse of the former but might see a fat, pink porker grunting around an open field *(right)*. Horses are far more numerous and range from sleek thoroughbreds to rare work horses with, in between, a huge population of hacks and ponies *(opposite top)* much loved by pony club members and country children.

Two-metre-high mesh fences are a sign of deer farming - a fast expanding industry. These hinds *(below)* are Wapiti/Red deer cross: nervous, watchful and easily spooked, quite unlike the tethered goat whose job is to graze the roadside but who takes time off to climb on to his hutch *(opposite below)* and watch the world go by.

The tedious work of driving a tractor across large paddocks is made easier by providing the farmer with a comfortable cab often equipped not only with telephone, radio, CD and cassette players, but also with laptop computer and GPS. Soil grading and windrow forming *(left)* is in progress preparatory to planting a potato crop; while *(below)* a tractor-drawn five-furrow plough works around a hilly South Island paddock.

It is claimed that aerial top-dressing was invented in New Zealand. It is certainly the most effective way to apply fertilizers to hill country. This aircraft *(opposite top)* is spreading lime/superphosphate on cattle country.

The flat plains of Canterbury, between the South Island alps and the Pacific are often watered by immense computer-controlled travelling irrigators *(opposite below)* that creep across the paddocks like alien creatures from another planet.

(Overleaf) Disk-harrowing breaks down the soil particles so that they will be ready for seed-drilling.

The farmer with his 'ute' full of dogs *(above)* awaits a mob of new shorn sheep which he and the dogs will head off and drive on to new pastures. Without the dogs, each of which has a special purpose, the flock would be virtually uncontrollable.

While New Zealand is as up-to-date as any farming country there still remain buildings from the nineteenth century such as this old barn *(below opposite)* north of Auckland.

Hives *(right)* in an open field suggest clover, and on a warm summer's day you'll hear the murmur of honey bees working low down among the purple and white flowers collecting nectar. Clover also does an important job fixing nitrogen to enrich soils whose grasses might later be cropped as silage in one continuous process where the grass is cut and thrown through the air into a hopper *(opposite top)* later to be stored, green, to ferment for winter livestock feed.

As an alternative to silage, winter feed for cattle, sheep and other grazing animals is made from hay, golden ripened meadow grasses which are harvested either into box-shaped bales which can be lifted by hand, or into large, round bales which can only be handled with the proper machinery. Big bales are often seen stored in barns *(opposite top)* or even in abandoned farmhouses, but more and more these days they are wrapped in plastic *(opposite below)*; these will probably be stacked in a convenient corner of a field.

On the fringes of most towns and cities, where the town meets the country, market gardens flourish. Many sell their produce at the gate *(above)* offering not only the expected fruit and vegetables but also eggs, flowers, fruit drinks, jams, honey, marmalade and other preserves.

Rural roadside signs warn motorists of cattle and sheep, school buses, one-way bridges, fords, railway crossings: 'Ducks Crossing' *(left)* is not as unusual as it might seem!